T0129896

MEMORIES
OF A
LITTLE SMALL TOWN
GIRL FROM SOUTHERN
WISCONSIN
BORN IN 1938

Judith Ellen Dixon Schlecht

MEMORIES OF A LITTLE SMALL TOWN GIRL FROM SOUTHERN WISCONSIN BORN IN 1938

iUniverse books may be ordered through booksellers or by contacting:

iUniverse
1663 Liberty Drive
Bloomington, IN 47403
www.iuniverse.com
1-800-Authors (1-800-288-4677)

Because of the dynamic nature of the Internet, any web addresses or links contained in this book may have changed since publication and may no longer be valid. The views expressed in this work are solely those of the author and do not necessarily reflect the views of the publisher, and the publisher hereby disclaims any responsibility for them.

Any people depicted in stock imagery provided by Thinkstock are models, and such images are being used for illustrative purposes only. Certain stock imagery © Thinkstock.

ISBN: 978-1-5320-2157-2 (sc)
ISBN: 978-1-5320-2158-9 (e)

Print information available on the last page.

iUniverse rev. date: 05/15/2017

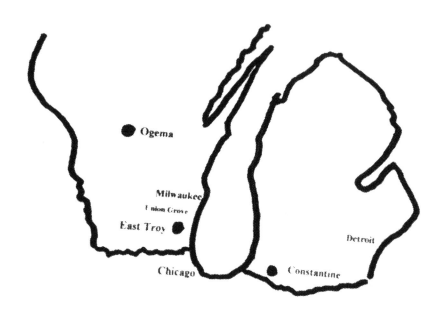

PREFACE

January 10, 2016

After reading my friend Phyllis Coe's autobiography <u>Life on an Ontario Farm</u> I decided it might be nice to tell my childhood story as I remember my early life and things about my family told to me (mostly by my mother).... rather like a verbal history. The memories will not be in sequence because one thought would lead to another random thought. Maybe the kids and grand kids might be interested when they get older! (Probably not, but I enjoyed doing it.)

My uncle Blair who still lives in Wisconsin has so much knowledge of the Dixon/Bowers family history! He was my reliable source for much family background information and generously emailed me facts off and on for over a year. My Aunt Vaughn who lives in California helped me remember even more details about the times of our growing up.

I was born in Burlington, Wisconsin Nov. 7. 1938. My father (Cecil John Dixon) liked to tease my Mother (Mildred "Milly" Motley Dixon) by saying they were married, Nov. 20th as though it was after I was born. (But they were married in 1937. Interestingly enough Mom was 20 years, 8 months, 18 days old when she was married, and I was exactly the same age when I married.!) At first Mother and Dad lived in a rented cottage at Booth Lake near East Troy Wisconsin. Then they rented a little house in East Troy. I have photos of me with my aunt Joyce at that rented house as well as a four generation picture (Dad's maternal side).

At that time my dad was a chiropractor in a clinic in East Troy owned by Dr. Behrens. A few years later he bought the practice when Dr. Behrens started a larger clinic and spa in Waukesha. Before he and mother had married Dad had a very small practice in Jefferson, Wisconsin and was pleased to have 4 or 5 patients a day. It was a tough start.

While Dad and his friend Stewart Howell (a fellow graduate from Lincoln Chiropractic College) worked with Dr. Behrens they liked to play tricks on the nurse assistant who Dad said was rather a pest. One day they were supposed to be checking urine samples. They held up the test tubes (containing white wine, maybe) in front of the nurse and pretended to taste them and said "Oh yes this one tastes like it has albumen. This one has too much salt." Dad said she ran out of the room and left them alone from that time on.

Dad had graduated from high school when he was 16. As a matter of fact his mother had given birth to his brother Blair the night he graduated from high school.

(This brother, Blair was my favorite uncle and he gave me the wings from his Air force uniform when I was a girl.) Dad already had 2 younger brothers (Dean and Merle) and a younger sister (Joyce) at this time. Dad went to Normal School to become a teacher but disliked teaching school very much. (It was a country school including all grades.) He was able to borrow money from a chiropractor in Union Grove and according to my mother... his own mother (a secret stash?) So he went to Indianapolis to the Lincoln School of Chiropractic.

Mother's parents had been divorced when she was just a baby. I am sure this was something she was ashamed of when she was older and realized the other kids had two parents. She never told me her parents were divorced until I was probably in my 20's. Her father had died when she was 17. He had a heat stroke while he was gathering hay during an extremely hot summer when even cows were dying in the fields. I guess she thought there was no reason to tell me about the divorce. My father was dating Mother when her father died. He tells about her sadness in his diary.

My mother had lived on a farm that had been homesteaded near Ogema, a small town in central Wisconsin which was also a lumbering area. Like most neighbors her family, the Hammars, had a garden, milk cows and chickens. They baked their own bread, chopped their own wood. They loved to pick wild berries (but had to watch out for bears. Bears like blueberries too!) There was, of course a well for water and kerosene lamps. Her grandfather was a patriarch and loved to read. Her grandmother and their children did most of the farm work! Although the Hammars and their neighbors might be considered poor, my Mother said she never felt poor because they always had plenty to eat. Occasionally one of the uncles would shoot a deer or even a bear so dinner might include venison or bear meat stew.

Mother's mother was from a large Swedish family. Her name was Alfhild and was called Alfhie. She had 5 sisters: Anna, Sapho, Gerda, Julia and Adella. She also 4 brothers, Arthur, Ralph, Ben and Carl. Most still lived on the farm although Anna, Sapho, and Gerda had married and left. The men never married. Mother's colloquiums may have come from the Swedes. She had many sayings like "Sing before breakfast, cry before night" (This certainly kept the early morning noise level down!) Then there was "Bread and Butter" (go together?) a must say if something came between you and the person with whom you were walking (to prevent a fight). There were more.

Alfhild married Howard Motley, the brother of a fellow (Harlan Motley) who was married to a neighbor lady, Ebba. Harland and Howard Motley had homesteaded out West earlier, sold their property, made a little money and come back to Wisconsin.

Alfhie's new husband, Howard built a home a few miles down the road from the Hammars on County Road I. Evidently there was a quarrel and Alfie, pregnant with my mother, returned home and never went back. Mother later told me her father was a smart ass. He did come back to Ogema from time to time to visit her but I have the idea they were not close. Mother went to a one room school house. After grade school she would have had to travel several miles down the road and catch the train to the nearby town (maybe 6 or 7 miles) to go to high school. Many of the kids her age did that. They took the train, stayed in the hotel for the week, then went home for weekends. (Mother told me this.) Of course the roads were at times impassable with snow.

So it was decided she would go to live in Union Grove where her father had relocated years ago and stay with her father's sister and her husband. Their names were Aunt Mabel and Uncle Frank Higgins. She was to go to high school and help with chores. She went on the bus from Ogema by herself to Racine, somewhat near Union Grove. Reading her letters to her mother, I learned no one came to meet her for hours. How scary! She must have been only 13. However, from her letters and reminiscences she had good years and many friends in high school. (Mom and Dad remained friends with Union Grove friends until they or the friends died.) I think she met my Dad when she was 16 or 17. Dad was born in Oct. 1912 so was an "older man" (4 ½ years older.) He was very smitten! I think they met at a dance. They both loved to dance. Dad was going to Chiropractic School in Indianapolis and wrote to her every day. In those days people hitchhiked, and he did that as often as possible to get home to see her. Dad was a very good student getting mostly A's. I still have his Grey's Anatomy book (and love letters). Before they were married, Mother was a book keeper for a company in Racine.

Mom's Family's
Homestead in
Ogema, Wisconsin

Mom and her mother
Around 1919

Milly Motley's
High School Photo

Mom and Dad
while Dating
With Dad's
Brothers and
Sisters
Dean, Blair,
Merle, Joyce
and Vaughnnie
Mom and Dad

My Favorite Bonnie
and Clyde
Mom and Dad
dating years

Dad's graduation photo
Lincoln Chiropractic
College
January 1937

Mom's Glamour Shot
Probably 1936

November 20, 1937

Mom and Dad on vacation
At the Wisconsin Dells
Shortly after they were
married
Nice outfits!

And then there was me

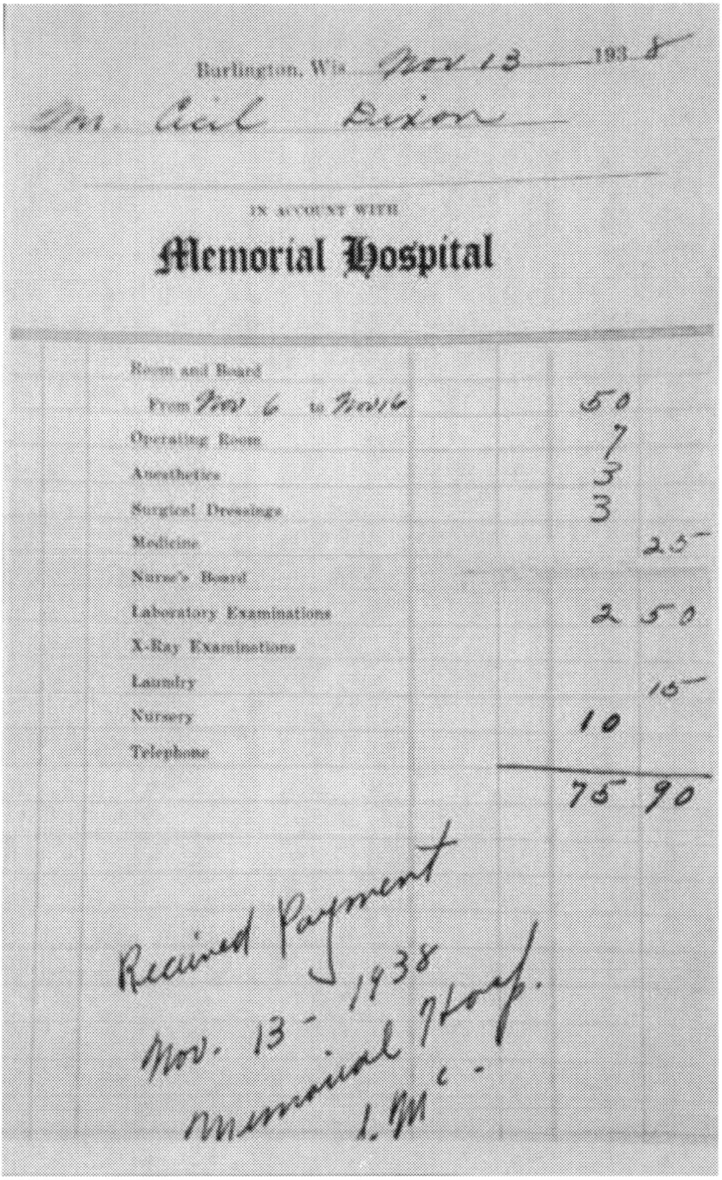

Burlington, Wis. Nov 13 193 8

Mr. Cecil Dixon

IN ACCOUNT WITH

Memorial Hospital

Room and Board		
From Nov 6 to Nov 16	5	0
Operating Room	7	
Anesthetics	3	
Surgical Dressings	3	
Medicine	2	5
Nurse's Board		
Laboratory Examinations	2	5 0
X-Ray Examinations		
Laundry		15
Nursery	1	0
Telephone		
	75	90

Received Payment
Nov. 13 – 1938
Memorial Hosp.
I. M c. –

Imagine! Cost of hospital stay
For Mother and Baby for 10 days
Was $75.90
No insurance in those days.

Four generation
Grandma Dixon
Great Grandpa and
Grandma Bowers with me
Dad

1939

I have memories surrounding the first home they bought when I was three or four. Mother had inherited a little money from her Uncle Frank and Aunt Mable. This money went toward buying a home in East Troy.

The memories I have of this first home they bought are vague but I do remember the neighbor children's swing set and the next door lady scaring me by telling me about "Bloody Tongue" living in what I suppose was her cistern. She was worried I would fall down in the hole and drown so she invented a monster being in there. I have a hazy recollection of my mother "disappearing" into the ceiling of the house one day. I was very frightened. (Actually there was a pull down stairs into the attic!) I remember Mom had cocker spaniels I played with. They shared their fleas with me. The dogs were named Big Boy and Lady D (for Dixon) A woman on the street murdered them by putting broken glass in hamburger and laying it out for them to find...how awful.

Big Boy and Lady D earlier had puppies. I remember going somewhere to sell the puppies and Mom having them on leashes. We did keep one of the pups (Brownie) who used to follow Dad as he drove his car around the town square after we moved to our second house. My aunt Vaughnie tells me that when Brownie got home one day right after following Dad he tried to walk up the basement steps but he too had been poisoned. He fell through the open steps. Dad said someone had put strychnine in meat which he ate on the way home. Vaughnie tells me Dad took out a big ad on the front page of the local newspaper addressing this horrible deed. We then had a collie sort of dog called Spike. He lived in the barn and would carry his pan in his mouth (by the handle) hoping for more food. (a REAL panhandler!) My Dad said someone stole him because he was a good hunting dog.

When I was probably five years old we moved to the large house that was my father's office as well as our home. (Dad had bought Dr. Behren's practice.) There had been 3 chiropractors and a nurse and now Dad was on his own. He worked every day often until nine o'clock but took Thursdays, Saturday afternoon and Sunday off (unless someone needed him, of course).

Our second house was a beautiful Victorian with a large yard and a circular driveway in back with a bird bath in the center. There was a real barn in which was kept a lot of junk and in which I ran a "library" with my own books one summer. I also decided to have a pet show that summer. I had determined the winner would be a baby goat that lived down the street. (Apparently goats were allowed in town. I know my parents had me drinking goat's milk, probably unpasteurized, when I was younger.) I was quite skinny and goat's milk was supposed to "fatten me up." Anyway, I was carrying the little goat to my own pet show when the goat threw his head back, piercing a hole in my cheek, just missing my eye. My mother ended the pet show right then and there which made me pretty mad.

This house was spacious. There was a big wraparound porch on the front. My Dad's office had a sizable waiting room with a staircase leading to our personal upstairs area (fun to slide down when no patients were around), a room where Dad did chiropractic adjustments and 2 rooms for heat treatments, etc. Our private downstairs area consisted of a living room (with a pretty fireplace... great for hanging Christmas stockings) a dining room and a large kitchen with a breakfast booth. I loved the booth as I had the inside seat where the windows were and got to slide under my father's legs to run outside after lunch. There were racks above the booth where Mom kept some special dishes. Speaking of Christmas...one year Mom and Dad got a risqué record from some friends. They played it quite a bit and somehow I memorized it and sang it to the class (4th or 5th grade) The teacher hadn't known what I was going to sing and I didn't know what the words meant... of course my parents were horrified when they found out!

The house had a large basement under most of the house. Where it wasn't finished (under the kitchen) was a dirt floor. We had a stray cat that adopted us and lived there. She had only three good legs, with the fourth leg sort of just attached. I think she had kittens in that space. My Dad had a work bench in the finished part of the basement and over the work bench often hung stretchers with muskrat hides, even sometimes mink hides. My father trapped these animals and sold the hides. Of course it was cruel but I don't think many people considered that. Beulah Woline, a friend and neighbor of Mom and Dad's told me a few years ago (yes, she was still alive in her 90's and we had lunch in East Troy) that my parents used to leave me with her at 6 am and Mom went with Dad to collect his traps. Dad also did a lot of duck hunting and I still have a few old decoys. (I remember when we were living in Constantine, Michigan in the 1950's Mom went duck hunting with Dad and their friend Foster Daugherty and she came home with some buck shot in her butt. I never found out how that happened but I think that was the last time she went duck hunting.)

The upper level had 5 bedrooms. During the war, rentals were scarce so my parents made an apartment on the second floor with a bedroom and kitchen. The apartment was rented to some friends, Lola and Hardie LeSauer. (After the war the kitchen was kept in the apartment and it was sort of a playroom for me.) Once I frightened the LeSaures at night because I came into their bedroom while sleepwalking. Luckily that didn't occur when I had the screaming nightmare about a large bear coming for me...a nightmare caused by eating apples at night according to my mother. (Who knew?!)

There was a turret in the attic of the house that was really cool and there was an Ouija board up there. My mother told me never to touch it. (I think they had fooled around with it with friends and it was considered to be calling on spirits of the dead.) Mom did the cleaning of the house and I remember her shaking her dust mop outside from the second floor balcony of the upstairs. It is a funny memory. Another funny memory is of my sidekick Kay Francis and me digging up moss, making a little rug on the lawn with the moss and just sitting on it (until we got bored).

Across the street was the Methodist Church we attended. Mother let me draw pictures during the service. My Sunday school teacher was Beulah, Mother's friend. She taught us to "put on our (pretend) gloves" as we left. As we pulled on the fingers of the gloves we were to say "Do unto others" (each word went with a finger) "as you... would they do unto you," Then you buttoned 3 buttons under each glove and said: "Love one another," and "God is Love." One Sunday I was to sing a duet with some other girl and she quit before the service. So I sang a solo. It was 'I come to the Garden Alone." I still love that song.

Shortly after we moved to this home my Grandmother Hammar (Mother's mother) came to visit. She wore long dresses. This is the only time I saw her except when I was very little and Mom took me to the Hammar's old farmhouse in Ogema. I was too young to remember that. (I have photos of our stay there though.) I think my Mother's family was somewhat reclusive. Mother's Grandfather was known to be a "freethinker" (considered an atheist) so probably wasn't in agreement with many in the community. (Many Swedes are Lutheran). I think my mother respected her grandpa very much but she did say that he sat around reading while the rest of the family did the chores. As I mentioned these 40 acre farms had been homesteaded so the family lived quite far out from the little town and way off the road.

Additionally, being Swedish, they were naturally reserved. There were secrets also. My mother's aunt had a boy born out of wedlock and the child died right away. The aunt, Julia, Mother's favorite, died shortly thereafter of something they called milk fever. (Some of her sisters knew who the father was of the child, and somewhere in the many letters I kept, was his name.) Mother was heartbroken. My mother wanted to name me Julia, but my father wouldn't hear of it (bad luck?)

Another letter I found in the hundreds of letters kept by my mother was very wrenching. It was a letter written by my mother to her mother begging her to come to Union Grove to attend her wedding. Apparently my Grandmother didn't feel comfortable about her appearance because Mother wrote she would lend her mother her own fur coat (it was November...I was surprised Mother could afford one, but perhaps they weren't so expensive then) and she would come get her or meet the bus. My grandmother was deaf, so I am sure that was an issue for her around strangers. Mother told me once how angry she got at her mother when she was a child because she was pointing to an airplane (how rare could that have been in the early 1920's!) and her mother wouldn't look up. Mother had to make all the arrangements for her own wedding

Another tragedy that occurred on the farm was when one of her Uncles (Carl) who was a twin (Arthur), shot himself. He had tuberculosis and left a long letter for the newspaper saying there was to be no question as to why he had done it (he hadn't wanted to infect the others in his family). Mother told me her grandmother, Carl's mother, was never the same again and she died that year. She had born ten children.

We visited another aunt later, Aunt Adella, in Montana when I was 13. They only had well water which was kind of funny because she had won a washing machine which they couldn't use. Advertising companies used to have rhyming jingle contests in those days, and I think she often won things. Mother wrote to Aunt Adella often. By the time we moved to Michigan only Uncle Ben, an alcoholic, my Grandmother and a sister (Gerda) were left on the old farm. Mother seldom went back to Ogema and consequently I never really knew my Grandma Hammar. Since Mother's mother was deaf and had been since Mother was a girl (I don't know what caused it) of course there were no phone calls, but there were many, many letters. At Christmas we always prepared a very special box for the three left on the farm. Since I never really knew my grandma Hammar, I have some guilt about this, as I feel as an adult I could have made an effort to see her, but was busy with my life and it didn't even occur to me. There was never a grave marker for Aunt Julia or Aunt Gerda. As a sort of atonement I had two markers made for them and placed at the Hammar family gravesites in Ogema.

Soon after we moved to the "new" house Ruby came to live with us. She was a high school girl unhappy living on a nearby farm. She helped Mom take care of me and with the housework. After she finished high school she was also Dad's assistant. There was a man who had a crush on her and brought her chocolates every week. It was war time, so chocolate was quite special! I think she lived with us several years. She got engaged to a farmer but broke up with that fellow when she found out she was to be his gem (Ruby) in his crown for heaven after she converted to Catholicism for him.

Ruby's fiancé had given her this really neat dressing table with a little cloth skirt that had legs that opened so you could sit at it. I thought it was really wonderful and "inherited" it when she found another future husband. Ruby said Harold Mueller just wanted her for herself, so she needn't convert although he was also Catholic. (She might have converted later) He took her away to California. (Maybe she just didn't want to be a farmer's wife.) We always kept in touch with Ruby and visited her in Livermore California when we went West in 1953.

Ruby babysat me when Mom and Dad went partying. Mom's friend (Cec) told me Mom used to go to Cec and Hap's tavern some evenings and wait for Dad to finish work so they could have some drinks. I also remember a big costume party at our house. As the guests came in Mom had costumes ready. They had lots of crazy friends. On Sundays they bowled and we kids ran all over the bowling alley. Mother was a good bowler and when we lived in Constantine, Michigan Mom went to Detroit with her team and won three trophies. I still have them. One has a broken arm. Mom said Dad broke it because she was the better bowler. Ha! I still have her bowling shirt also.

On Saturday nights (I suppose before my parents went out) Ruby and Mother gave me a bubble bath while we listened to the latest "Hit Parade" on the radio. The bathroom was really large with black tile and had a tub and separate shower...which Mother wouldn't let people use...she said it leaked but I think it was just hard to clean. It was so cold in the mornings before school! We had a dangerous looking electric coil heater in that bathroom to help keep us warmer for dressing. Of course I listened to that program on the radio where the announcer had the girls and boys racing against one another to dress quickly and you could send in the mail for a secret message ring. My ring had a red plastic top with a slide in which to hide the secret message. There were hot water radiators throughout the house. When she came to visit Grandma Dixon liked to sit on the ones in the dining room that had covers.

When I was about seven, little boys became interesting. Girls and boys would have little gangs against one another. I think we just ran to and away from the boys. One day I came in for lunch and Mother asked me who I was fighting with (wrestling I suppose) and I said: "That is my boyfriend, Bobby Shinkenburger." That name has stuck with me to this day. He had red hair. Lots of boys in East Troy had red hair, as many were Irish or German. Since there were so many Irish families, the Catholic Church was very dominant in town. When my best friend Kay had her first communion, I was so envious of her pretty white dress, white Bible and little gold cross.

I also remember being very popular one winter. The girls were supposed to make snowballs at recess for the boys who ganged up on one another. I had red gloves. As the gloves got wet they turned the snowballs pink!

We had 2 dogs that got hit by cars, Riley, a Springer Spaniel who had eight puppies including one we kept (Coalie) a beautiful dog named for her shiny black coat. Coalie moved to Michigan with us. Riley had neuralgia in her legs after she was hit but still had the puppies.

The story about the puppies is that the neighbor's dog dragged his dog house by the chain to come to our yard when Riley was in heat and Dad let her out since the male dog was so adamant...Mother was very angry about it but the puppies were really adorable...(half Springer, half Labrador Retriever). Later my parents told me they had taken Riley to a farm so she could run free but of course years later I figured they had put her to sleep because her legs got so bad.

We had white rabbit pets named Susie and Thumper and later a grey rabbit named Squirley. One winter Squirely got loose from his outdoor hutch and was nearly frozen. Mom gave him a shot of whiskey and he was revived. From then on he lived free in the basement. Sometimes I would massage his little temples. One time as I was massaging his temples he got so relaxed he peed on me and the couch.

We later had a male cat that had a large head and was named! Fat Head. He also moved to Michigan with us. He slept in the laundry room when not looking for lady cats. Neighbors teased Mom about calling my father Fathead when she was calling the cat.

We often visited Mom and Dad's old friends and Dad's family in Union Grove, which was only 25 miles away. My great grandparent's house was inundated with little kids because my Uncle Merle and Aunt Helen moved in with their 3 little children after the war. Uncle Merle had been a paratrooper in World War Two. He had broken his leg in training but continued in the service. He was in the famous 82nd division which saw combat in Sicily, Salerno (a night jump!) and Normandy where there were 5,245 paratrooper casualties. The next mission was in Holland and finally he was engaged in the famous Battle of the Bulge in France. 19,000 American soldiers died in this conflict so we were lucky Uncle Merle survived. The 82nd was then assigned to General Patton and he dubbed them the All Americans and Flying Eagles. Patton had great respect for these paratroopers. The division was assigned to Berlin for occupation duty. Merle sent post cards to my parents from France. He wanted to name my cousin Victoria because she was born on Victory over Europe Day, May 8, 1945 but she is named Sandra!

I inherited an upright piano from that home owned by my great grandparents. It was graced with little teeth marks on the keyboard. I hated taking piano lessons and practicing scales...I later took flute lessons so I could be in the school band. I played piccolo too. I had always wanted to use the snare drums. Well, I did get to carry the large bass drum in a marching parade once!

The piano had been my grandmother's. My uncle Blair tells me she taught herself to play and was quite good. He says the family would gather around the piano on Sundays and sing hymns after my aunt Joyce and Grandma had put dinner in the oven. The family liked to harmonize. My great grandparents lived next door and also across the street from a school yard which had a really cool jungle gym. My aunt Vaughnnie, who is only 5 years older than I am, always took me there when we visited. Grandpa was a carpenter. It was rough going during the depression with little construction going on. Just before the United States got in World War Two, Grandma and Grandpa moved to South Chicago because Grandpa found employment at the Navy Yard. After the war there was plenty of work for carpenters.

I stayed with my Grandma in Chicago a few times. I remember her yelling down from upstairs, "Juder (she called me that) what are you doing?" because I liked to sneak and rub sugar so hard into bread it became solid. One time she took me to the Chicago Zoo and we came around a corner and there was the famous Gorilla, "Bushman." He was Huge and Scary. I also learned about stop lights there because one was on the busy corner of their house and a police woman stood there at times. (No stop lights in East Troy!) Many times Grandma also let me knead the oleo. This "margarine" was in a plastic pouch with an encapsulated yellow button of dye that when squeezed and massaged would make the shortening look like butter. This could not be sold in Wisconsin, "The Dairy State"!

When I was older we usually spent Christmas at my Grandma and Grandpa's in Chicago. I believe this was after we moved to Michigan. I do remember all my aunts and uncle and cousins (except those from Tennessee) came for Christmas dinner. Once about 8 of us cousins stayed overnight Christmas Eve and slept on blankets in the dining room. It was fun. I eventually had 23 first cousins, all alive today.

My Uncle Merle, Aunt Helen and 5 kids were living in the basement apartment in my grandparent's house in Chicago at this time. One Christmas Helen got very drunk and was crying and crying because she was remembering the Christmas when she was a little girl and her younger sister had burned to death because the Christmas tree had fallen on her. At that time people used real candles to decorate the trees. The parents had left Helen, her brother and her little sister alone as they went to milk the cows. The tree tipped over and that tragedy happened. The parents blamed Helen...how cruel... and often there would be this remorse for her.

One Christmas when I was about 12, Uncle Blair and Aunt Nancy, Aunt Vaughn, my Grandma, my Dad and I went downtown to Marshall Field's to shop. We split up and were supposed to meet at "the clock." Well, there were two large clocks, so the two groups were waiting at different places. When we finally got home we found Grandpa had decided to put down new tile in the kitchen as a surprise. He had drunk <u>way</u> too much wine and left black goop used to stick down the tiles all over the floor. (Of course Grandma had just cleaned for company coming.) Poor Grandma just sat down and wept.

One time my grandmother got robbed by a young black man when she left from work at Sears. The police asked her to describe him. She said he was dark with brown eyes! My grandfather also got hurt by some young black men but he remained unprejudiced. In later years when my grandparents were living at Birch Lake, Michigan, an adult group decided to bring black children by bus from South Bend, Indiana to the public landing there. It was probably a protest group, as this occurred during the 60's. Some residents wanted to put up a barbed wire fence, but Grandpa said the children had every right to swim there. My Mother said when Grandpa was a young man his father-in-law wanted him to join the Ku Klux Klan in Union Grove. (My Uncle Blair says this is not true but where would my mother get that idea if Grandpa hadn't told her?) Mom said Grandpa said: "No, he wasn't going to dress in white sheets." I think maybe the Ku Klux Klan was against Catholics in Union Grove because there were very few black people there anyway.

There is an interesting story about my Grandma Ethel's mother, Ellen Bowers. She was watching the Wright Brother's air exhibit at the fairgrounds near Milwaukee when the plane crashed into the stands and she was hit. Great Grandmother was in bed for a year recovering and received compensation which she and her husband John Bowers used to buy a farm. Ellen Bower's mother was Ellen O'Shawnasee who supposedly kissed the blarney stone before she immigrated to America from Kerry Ireland. (Probably true, because the family seems very much full of blarney.) Ellen O'Shawnasee married Great Great-Grandfather Nobes, who enlisted in the Civil War in 1861 when he was 23. (My uncle Blair tells me Great Grandfather Nobes was under 5'5" tall) He was wounded in 1862 and thereafter was a drummer for battles and parades. A famous eagle called Old Abe associated with the 8th Wisconsin regiment often rode on Great Great Grandpa's drum and was cared for by him. The bird's body was eventually preserved and kept on display in the Wisconsin State House until a fire destroyed the building.

After Great Grandpa and Grandma Bowers gave up farming, Great Grandpa became the mayor of Union Grove for many years (Interesting, as my Dad became mayor of the little town of Constantine in the 1950's.) Great Grandpa was one of ten children. <u>His</u> father (Isaac) was born in Nottingham, England in 1826 and had left England to settle in Sylvania, Wisconsin. Six years later he sent for his wife, Sarah Ann Lee of Lancaster. I was very fortunate to know those great grandparents.

However, I didn't know my Great Grandfather Dixon. He and Great Grandmother Dixon were also farmers but later bought a shoe shop in Union Grove. I do have a vague memory of seeing Great Grandma Dixon, a short stocky woman. My father's uncle was named Price. This was his mother's maiden name. One summer we took a vacation up North at Uncle Price's lodge where he and his wife (Aunt Marge) had cottages to rent. We stayed several days in a houseboat on the lake. One day I saw a HUGE blood sucker in a tin can on the way to the lake. It wasn't there the next day so I thought it had gone in the lake. I wouldn't swim anymore but didn't say why. Probably someone was actually saving it as bait to catch fish.

My aunt Vaughn, who as I said was only 5 years older than me, stayed with us at least one summer. (Mother said Grandma was going through "the change" and couldn't stand anyone.) So Vaughnie slept in my bed with me. This meant I couldn't leave my myriad of stuffed animals in the bed. I also had two large dolls, over 12" long, that usually also occupied the bed. These dolls had molded heads with eyes that could open and shut. One was fancy with yellow hair the other was a "plain Jane." I think I thought the "plain Jane" resembled me and so she was allowed to sleep next to me whereas Miss Fancy was not.

My bedroom had really wonderful wallpaper with a Mickey and Minnie theme. I still have a little piece. Mother and Dad were actually good wallpaper hangers! Dad did the pasting, Mother the hanging. One time they got in a fight while wallpapering. I was in the room and said if they didn't stop fighting I would leave. They ended up laughing. When Spring arrived I would hear the lovely soft cooing of doves each morning outside my bedroom window.

Vaughnie always drew an imaginary line in the (middle?) of the bed and if I went over the line she got to kick me. (Her rule) Perhaps this was a suppressed revenge. When her fifth birthday arrived Nov.8, 1938, she was told there was a big surprise for her. She was sure it was a pony! The surprise was a trip to the hospital to see baby Judy. She was <u>not</u> pleased.

Vaughnie taught me how to play jacks. We enjoyed having her stay and she liked Ruby as well. One summer when I was almost nine years old our parents decided to send Vaughnie and me to Memphis on the train (by ourselves!) to visit Aunt Joyce and Uncle Larry. We left from Chicago and stayed at least a week. Aunt Joyce was quite the trooper to let us visit because Cousin Janice was only 11 months old at the time. We were there during Fourth of July week. We were sent to the market with a dollar to buy a watermelon. On the way back Vaughn dropped the watermelon and it split in two. She really caught hell from Uncle Larry! Vaughnie and I have stayed close and she was my maid of honor at my wedding.

Sometimes when we went to Union Grove we would go on to see relatives of my Mother's father's in nearby Kansasville. These were the Voges. They lived on a farm and had older children...just one was close to my age, Mardel. They had a player piano which I found fascinating. They had many different songs on paper rollers that made the piano keys go up and down while the roller turned. The Voges did a lot of canning. I remember it being hotter than the devil in their kitchen and there was a circle of sticky yellow fly paper hanging from the ceiling with nasty dead flies stuck to it. Mother had a fear of me dying somehow or another because their youngest son, my age, had hung himself accidentally in the barn while getting eggs when he was probably about 5 years old. Another friend's child had drunk lye water (used for cleaning cow udders) and died. People seem to believe things "happen in threes" so Mother thought she should be watching out for me.

Les Voge was Cousin Ruth's husband. Les had an accident involving a bull which left him with two or three fingers missing on one hand. In later years our son John saw this and was pretty fascinated with that hand. Ruth had a really funny strident voice but she was a very nice person. Her daughter had the same voice! After Ruth died, Les sold the farm, went to an assisted living facility where he met another lady.... (Les was in his 80's) and married her....She died a few days after the wedding! I thought this was pretty funny, but now that I am 78, not so much! In the obit, the woman's family said how nice it was that they had met and married....HMM!

I remember going to a gathering of Mom's relatives near Union Grove and there was an aunt of hers there that had a goiter and her eyes bulged out...I was frightened of her. Lack of iodine (which causes goiters) was a problem in that area of the country. Now people, including me, take synthroid to prevent the problem.

One time when Mother and I were going to Union Grove, I misbehaved in the car. I wouldn't sit still. Of course this was before mandatory seat belts. Mother threatened to leave me behind. She put me out of the car and pretended to drive away! (Talk about abandonment issues!)

Actually, my parents were very kind to me. I only remember being spanked twice by my father. Once was when I was only around 6 or 7 I left with some older kids and Vaughnnie on a long walk and Mom and Dad didn't know where I was. (Vaughnie tells me we were throwing rocks at rats at the dump) The other time was when I ran out in front of the house (busy street) when a car was coming. My Dad was so upset he really spanked me and my mother said he might as well have let the car hit me. (Sometimes she could be sarcastic.) I was also given a very generous allowance for the times. I believe I started with fifty cents a week. At first I guess I didn't understand the concept because I ran out of money fast but they said was too bad and no more until next week. So I learned to budget at an early age. I saved. In fact I saved enough to buy a little camera that took 4" x 4" photos and a Mickey Mouse watch (wish I had that for Antique Roadshow!) However, my parents gave me the watch for Christmas so I didn't have to buy it.

I also once bought a baseball glove with money I had saved. I think this surprised my parents because I never played baseball. I probably wanted it because boys had them and I was rather envious of boys. It seemed they got to do more activities and have more fun. If I saw a boy climb a tree I would climber higher. (Very competitive... and I loved to climb trees and swing from the branches.)

Most children today start kindergarten when they become five. Our town at that time did not have kindergarten offered and we started first grade at age six. There were a bunch of tall bushes near the school and my house was only a block and a half from school. My friend Kay and I would set up house in those bushes and use stick brooms to sweep our dirt "floor" while we watched the school kids. I liked school. In truth I liked it so much I didn't come home for lunch one day (no school lunches then!). I was having fun swinging on the monkey bars and along came my mother, <u>very</u> mad, and I think carrying a switch but she didn't smack me with it. I suppose she had been worried.

In school our desks had ink wells. We actually used quill pens. One day a friend and I put chalk in a full inkwell and there was big trouble. I also got in trouble one day in 3rd or 4th grade when I brought in a jar of lady bugs and accidently broke it. The bugs got all over the classroom! Eventually we were to buy bottles of ink that had their own little ink wells. I don't think "fountain" pens that drew the ink into them were made until quite a bit later.

One of the most exciting things in school was Halloween. Every class would have a costume contest and parade. One year my Mom made me a really great clown outfit. She wasn't much for sewing so it was a pretty big deal. Guess who won...Gloria Swoboda, with a stupid dime store-bought costume....I thought the one my mother made was much better! Another big deal was Valentine's Day. Unbeknownst to Mom, I volunteered to make the Valentine box. It was the coolest one ever, because she decorated a big round box my dad got supplies in....Up until then Valentine's boxes had always just been square. When we were about to move to Michigan (I was just beginning sixth grade) my class gave me a farewell party.

A boy named Melvin said he would always keep his Dixie cup to remind him of me (I was occasionally called Dixie).

The biggest deal in East Troy was the Fourth of July celebration. The Lion's Club sponsored the celebration. It lasted three days, and there were carnival rides, parades, bingo games, dart games, etc. In fact I won at Bingo 2 out of 3 games so they then decided I was too young to play! However I got to keep the lamp I had won during one of the games and I held on to it for years. The parade was very elaborate with bands from Milwaukee, decorated bikes and ponies to ride. I wasn't on a pony and someone noticed the Meany boys both had ponies so they made the younger boy get off saying both shouldn't have a pony and they gave me his pony. (I bet because my dad was a very active Lion member) Of course that Meany boy was so mad, and I really don't blame him. (We gave him one of Riley's beautiful puppies later so I think that made up for it.)

A couple that were really good friends with my parents while we were living in Wisconsin was Bernice and Harold Powles. They lived in Union Grove. After high school Mother and her friend Ruth Kortendick rented a room from the Powles. They were quite the characters. Harold was known as "Toad." I guess because he was rather squatty and had a round face. He had a machine shop in the barn that was just behind their house. Bernice made wonderful greasy donuts every Friday. Harold's mother lived with them and I think that was a pain for Bernice. "Grandma" made appliquéd tea towels and sold them to Marshall Field's. I have some she gave me for a wedding present. The towels are decorated with Orphan Annie in a red dress doing various tasks for each day of the week. Bernice always wrote funny letters to Mom and had lots of crass, newsy, hysterical comments about the people they all knew. I stayed in touch with Bernice until she died when she was about 103 years old.

When I was in 3rd or 4th grade we went on a trip out West with the Powles for a month. (Five in the car, women and child in back, of course) My teacher Mrs. Tess (a friend of my parents) said I could take the time out of school because I would learn more on the trip than in school. I took work books along. I got carsick. (My parents didn't realize for years I needed glasses.) I remember the Indians in Arizona running to the car to sell us stuff and brown bugs in our motel room. I remember going to the San Diego Zoo and Tijuana, Mexico. In Tijuana Mom bought us really neat jackets with appliqué. (Hers was white and black, mine was colorful and both were banded with blanket stitching) I wish I had hers now but it must have gotten moth-eaten because Mother typically never threw anything away.

Kay Francis Spiegelhoff and me

My best friend in East Troy was Kay Francis Spiegelhoff. Her parents and my parents were friends. We were both only children. Kay's dad called her Pumpkin and my dad called me Peanut. Kay was 5 months younger than I was. Kay was a beautiful child with big brown eyes and blond hair. I was a pretty ordinary looking little girl with (I think) rather a cherubic face! One reason

I think our Mom's bonded was because they both had a child that was stillborn. Kay's parents had a tavern downtown named Hap's Tavern. Kay's grandpa sat on a bench there most all the time. He rented a room in the house across the street. Kay and I could play shuffle board and have Coca Colas in the back of the tavern. Hap and Cec (Kay's mom) lived over the tavern in a very nice apartment. Kay and I used to slide down the long front stairway, and we also had a "secret" entrance from the back alley... a little trap door in the door that lifted up from the back stairs and was usually unlocked. We once played "doctor" looking at one another's "parts" but I didn't like the game. We had another stupid game we played based on an evil fairy tale called Blue Beard where he cut off his wives heads...We revised the story to cut off their boobs and pretended to hang them on the wall on the way down the stairs.

Kay was sort of tricky and much more aggressive than I was. My mother had given me an old bracelet with pretty red stones in it. Kay really wanted it. She wanted me to trade for a dumb cardboard animal. I didn't want to do it so she kept adding more dumb stuff until I finally gave in. Mother was quite mad at me about that. Kay's mom had one of those fox head shawls we loved to look at and pretend we would wear.

Kay and I did some crazy things. One day we climbed out on tree limbs to a little island on the river near town. We had some red paint. We painted the island and had to swing back to land again on the tree limbs. One Christmas just the two of us went all over town singing Christmas carols. We were only about 9 years old. That would be unheard of today but our town was only 1,000 people and most people knew everyone else and felt safe.

There was a town "square" that had a band stand where there were concerts on Saturday nights and the kids ran all over the place. There was a very pudgy bulldog that wandered around looking to be petted and begging for treats. Everyone knew her and her name was Gentle Julia.

I can think of five taverns in the 4 short streets around the square, but only remember one grocery store. (Surely there must have been two!) Mom and Dad went to restaurants frequently. Usually I went along. I suppose it wasn't too difficult taking one child and I was actually well behaved. (There was some pressure I think on my parents that I not be perceived as a "spoiled only child." They were strict but I didn't want for anything.) I recall ordering frog legs for dinner one time. I believe there was a discussion about it being an expensive meal but Dad said, "Oh, let her have them." They were good, too!

My parents often ate at the historic Cobblestone Hotel in East Troy. They would send me with quarters (dimes?) to the cigarette machine to buy their cigarettes. They smoked Camels. I would wonder why they didn't smoke Pall Malls. The slogan on the Pall Mall cigarette package was "Wherever Particular People Congregate." I wondered if my parents were not particular people!

My father was quite overweight. He would often try to diet. To encourage him, my mother once decided she wouldn't cook desserts for awhile. She liked to eat sweets herself but would "sacrifice" to help him. One day she went down town and caught him in one of the restaurants eating a big piece of pie with ice cream. She was so mad she came home and baked her favorite chocolate cake with thick fudge icing. (my favorite too) Maybe she and I ate it all!

I don't recall much about the war years except for seeing the occasional soldier and listening to the lovely sentimental ballads written at that time. Being a small town, I think there was not much rationing of sugar or meat there but we did save tin cans and the "tin foil" from our gum wrappers and bought war bonds at school.

The town had a movie theatre and we went to movies without our parents all the time. There was something unusual in the theatre called "love seats." These were double seats with no arm rests in between. Once the theatre was so full I had to sit with someone I didn't know and that was really yucky. There were very romantic movies with beautiful songs. Of course everyone loved Judy Garland singing "Clang, Clang, Clang went the Trolley" in "Meet me in Saint Louis" in 1944. And of course I fell in love with Dana Andrews, a war pilot in "The Best Years of Our Lives."

When I was 7 or 8 my parents bought me a bike. (I was mad that Kay got hers before I did and I was older!) She had an American Flyer (as did the neighbor Hardaker kids whose parents owned a hardware store and sold bikes). I just had a Montgomery Ward bike but mine was really nice because it had a solid center piece. I could stand on the seat with one leg, hold the handle bars and float my other leg out like a ballet dancer (I thought). I had that bike until I was in high school and painted it sea foam green.

Kay and I were in Brownie Scouts. Mom was a Scout leader and my dog Riley was our mascot. When we were ten we went to Girl Scout camp at Lake Geneva. It rained the entire time. We stayed in tents and although our cots had mosquito netting it didn't help much and we were covered in welts when our moms came to get us. They were very late. They had stopped at a tavern on the way and said they got the pickup time wrong. Hmm.

Another year we took dancing lessons...tap and ballet. The lessons were in the basement of the grade school. One day during our lesson, the basement filled with smoke and the fire department came. For some reason Kay and I ran into the high school section (because no one was looking and we could) and started yelling "Fire, Fire." (There was no fire in the high school section...it was just fun to do) Later it came out that the fire had been started by one of the high school kids.

One year Mom and Dad got a brand new "step down" Hudson...a new concept. The car seemed to have lots of problems and Mother and I spent many Saturdays in Milwaukee at the dealer's repair shop. I liked that because I always got to buy a new Nancy Drew mystery book with my allowance when we were in Milwaukee. I loved to read and the only library we had in East Troy was upstairs above some store. As I recall I read every Oz book there was.

Going to Milwaukee was fun. If you were going to get new shoes you could stick your feet with the shoes on in a machine and you could see your feet inside the shoes. Of course X-ray exposure isn't too good for feet but we didn't get new shoes very often.

Mother told me that when I was very young and while we were going up the back stairs of the Gimbles Department Store in Milwaukee I was horrified when I saw a black lady ironing clothing on a landing (to be hung on the racks). I asked my Mother what had happened to her face...I was evidently very worried!

One summer I remember the whole family had to take afternoon naps and we could not go to the town pool (the pool was really pathetic and small anyway, since there were lots of lakes nearby and we could even bike a few miles away to Booth Lake) There was an epidemic of polio and some thought that polio was spread in the pools. The little girl next door did get polio and had to wear a brace for her shorter leg. We didn't go to the lakes much that summer and I really missed that. One year the coach had taken kids on the school bus to Booth Lake several days a week. I remember two boys (I liked them and wanted to impress them) were dunking and holding me under the water. It was happening under the dock and the coach couldn't see this. I kept saying "Doesn't hurt me!" (Stubborn) until I finally felt like I would drown and I "hollered Uncle."

Often my mother took a bunch of us girls to that lake. There were two huge slides made of metal. I can still remember how hot they were as I slid down! The "second" slide was out deeper, and one day we decided to take Kitty Burns (who couldn't swim) out there in an inner tube. My mother saw us doing that and freaked out! I loved to swim and dive and when Mother was ready to leave I would call, "Only one more dive, Mother." (Again and again)

Occasionally on Sundays my parents would play golf. I was allowed to go along and (!) wash the golf balls. Many Sundays we went fishing. I would take comic books in case I got bored (which I did). While my pole was dangling in the water and I wasn't looking my Dad would sneak a fish from the bucket onto my pole, then say, "Judy, look at your bobber," and I would pull up a bluegill. In June, before church we would get out early to cut asparagus along the roads, where it grew wild. We got out early to beat the other pickers! Sometimes we went out to our friends the Woline's cabin in the woods where there were lots of wild flowers. The woods were named "Skunk Hollow." Now there is a big outdoor concert hall nearby where the Rolling Stones and other bands have played.

When I was probably almost eleven, six of us girls had a little gang. We were allowed to ride all over town and even out of town. Kay and I were the oldest. I do remember we rode to one of the girl's farm house where there was a barn and the brother of one of our gang was in the barn. He told Jeanie Hardacker, one of my friends, to take off her bluejeans. We thought he was nuts. (The is the only recollection I have of sexual "escapades" in East Troy unless you could count making a design in snow that some thought looked like bird wings, and one boy thought looked like a fanny.) Unfortunately we suffered from a siege of pyromania. We began to go to some little sand dunes outside of town, dig holes and light fires which was pretty safe, but we graduated to biking to a woods about two miles from the center of town where we started a brush fire which we could not control. Kay started screaming for her father, Lou Zeske screamed for her mother, Rita Hardaker and the other friend started beating at the fire with their coats, and Jeanie and I biked to a nearby farm for help. As I passed some bird's ground nests, I worried about the eggs getting burned. The farmers thought they had put the fire out, but in the night I heard fire trucks and we were in trouble. I lied to my parents and said Jeanie started the fire, when in fact we both lit the matches. About a year later while living in Constantine, I woke up screaming and confessed to my parents that I had also lit matches...conscience rules!

1943 Our beautiful Victorian home in East Troy Wisconsin
on Main Street
The post card says C.J. Dixon, Chiropractor,
Naturopath. Dad's office was in front.

Thumper the rabbit and me
1943

Mom is Maid of Honor
At Aunt Joyce and Uncle Larry's wedding
December 29, 1945 Memphis, Tennessee
Larry was in the service

Kay and Me in my back yard getting
ready to go to Booth Lake, 1944

Vaughnnie, me and Kay
Probably summer 1945

Grandma Dixon
She loved her hats!

Mom
Styles of the 40's
Wartime years

Lambing time at Rhoda's farm
Just outside East Troy limits 1946

Me with little
neighbor Carol
Hardarker
1946

Girls Scouts 1948
Bottom row, left side,
Rita Hardaker
Bottom row, right
side, Me and Riley our
mascot
Kay with Kitty Burns
behind her
Mother was the
Scout leader

Beautiful Coalie
1948 or 1949

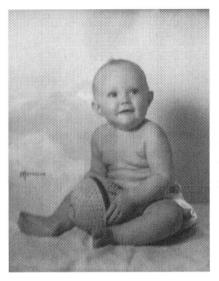 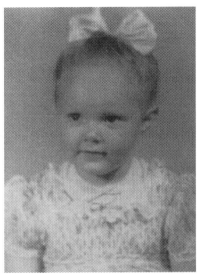

Judy through the years...

 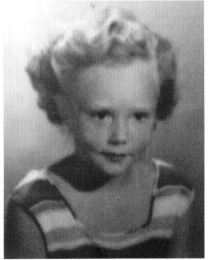

Kay Francis (I still call her that) remained my friend even after we moved to Constantine, Michigan. One time my mother was "called back" to Ogema and she didn't want me to go with her because she was to "rescue" her drunken uncle from the taverns...her mother needed her help. I rode to East Troy with Mother where I was left to stay with Kay's family as Mom went on her way to Ogema. By now Kay could drive and we rode all over singing the popular Prudence and Patience song "Tonight you belong to me," at the top of our lungs. We went to Booth Lake where went as children. I can still remember the smell of that lake. We went to Lake Geneva as well where we met some friends of hers. We also drank some 3/2 beer...a new experience for me!

Kay had something to do one afternoon so her Dad (Hap) took me out to a bar and offered me a cocktail. (Yes, I was very under age, but after all Hap was known everywhere) He asked me if I wanted a Martini or Manhattan. I had no idea. He drank Manhattans so he ordered me a Martini... it was awful, so he gave me his Manhattan...my first cocktail and I didn't like that either, though I changed my mind in my 30's!

In the fall of 1949 we had moved to Constantine, Michigan. I was very sad and missed my friends. I made little plaques that said "Home is Where the Heart Is" and "Home Sweet Home." I was in 6th grade. When my mother took me to school the teacher said there was no room for me, that the class was full. My mother told her, "You better make room because we live here now." Mother didn't take much guff!

Constantine is located in the south west corner of the state along the Saint Joseph River and was established as a town in the early 1800's. Many homes were historic in character (not mine). Life seemed to be of a slower pace here than in East Troy. Perhaps because of the river the town had been part of the Underground Railroad leading to Detroit and Canada. One of my friends' homes had a secret staircase and a room under the floor of the carriage house where supposedly slaves were hidden. Before the Civil War many former slaves settled in the nearby town of Vandalia where Quaker abolitionists lived and welcomed them.

After we had been living in Constantine about a month, I became very ill. I remember it was strange I wasn't in my own bed. (By the way, I had scratched branding iron signs like Rocking R into the back of my bedstead with bobby pins.) My father finally called in his chiropractic friend, Dr. Howell, to consult and I was rushed to the hospital. I had an emergency operation because my appendix had ruptured. My father had waited a bit long and my mother was furious with him. She would never have forgiven him if I had died. (She said so!) I was lucky because penicillin had been discovered. I was supposed to lay still but after 5 days in the hospital I got out bed and tried to run when the nurses weren't looking. (Couldn't do it) Talk about stubborn! About this age I was going through the chubby stage. I was rather distressed while shopping because I was not heavy enough for dresses made for really chubby kids or slender enough for regular clothing. Eventually I slimmed down.

About age 12

The following summer was when we lost our beautiful Coalie. She had been our pet for several years and came with us from East Troy. I had let her off the leash in the back yard and she ran right out in front. The road was quite busy and she got run over by a truck. Of course I felt devastated. Mother really loved that dog but she didn't make me feel guilty. After Coalie got killed we had a wonderful little dog. My grandparent's cocker spaniel had an "affair" with a dachshund and we brought home one of the puppies. We named the puppy Sammy. Sammy was very sweet and very funny looking. He had long black hair, a straggly tail and quite short legs.

A few years later when we visited my Grandparents at Christmas, Sammy disappeared. Grandpa looked for at The Humane Society for weeks. Mother thought someone had snatched him from the fenced yard after we let him out. She said he would have made a nice Christmas present for a kid. I hope that is what happened but I missed him terribly.

I think losing these dogs as a child has me especially fearful of losing my pets. (However, after Sammy there was Gilbert the basset/beagle who lived to a ripe old age and was around after I got married.) So far in my adult life my many pets have lived <u>very</u> long. (one cat aged 22, one dog aged 17!) (Well, one canary died young)

One day when I was 13 my Dad surprised me (and shocked my mother) by bringing home a (horse!) The neighbor who lived behind our alley had horses and a stable. I had been pitching manure there for over a year to prove I would take care of a horse if my parents would buy me one. I had gone to horse shows with the neighbors. My Dad actually just walked him (Laddie) home through the alley. There was no stall set up for him so we had to make room in the barn right then. There is a photo of Laddie with Sammy and me astride. At first I had no saddle, just a bridle. I guess you could say Dad was impulsive!! I did teach Laddie to canter from a walk, required for showing, but never showed him. He was just my very nice horse. Once I was riding bareback and fell in front of him and he just stopped. One winter day when I took Laddie from the barn and was about to mount up for a ride he slipped on ice. He moved sideways. Suddenly his hoof (and weight) was on my foot. I pushed on him and hollered at him to no avail. He didn't understand. Finally I bit him on his flank. He was so startled he lifted his leg fast!

After we moved to Constantine I did make friends with classmates and neighbors. The Daugherty family lived across our back alley and had 5 children. Their daughter Joy was 5 months younger than I was and a grade behind. School was only 9 blocks away. My house was on her way so Joy would stop and we walked together for many years. (Some days if I dilly dallied too long she would go on ahead without me.) If it was cold or snowing we would trudge along wearing ugly rubber galoshes (not like the designer boots girls wear today). By the time we got to school there were ugly black rings on our legs. When I was a freshman in high school I dated a senior who usually drove us to school (until he graduated). Later we often got rides with fellows who had their own cars.

In Constantine the grade schools, junior high and high school were all in one building. When Joy was in 7th and I was in 8th we had a crush on a sophomore, Jerry Flatland. We figured out which classes he was taking and when they were. We tried to follow him around on breaks between our classes. He seemed to wonder why two chubby adolescent girls were stalking him. He was not pleased.

Joy's older brother, Roger, teased me all the time. He would pull the wings from flies to torment me and make me scream. I considered Davey, about 3 years younger than I was and the twins who were about 4 years old, my wished-for younger brothers. These twins were quite a handful. I was told that their mother, Jean (who already had 3 children) fainted in the doctor's office when the doctor told her she was to deliver twins.

That was just the beginning. There was a gas station on the corner of our street. The owner of this gas station (Hank) was fond of the boys (Danny and Dennis) and they spent a lot of time at the station. When Denny was about five years old he fell in the pit where the oil was emptied. What a mess! Another time the twins put snow in the opening to the oil tank. It froze. No delivery for awhile! Later there was a problem with the gas pipe so they dug the pipe up. It was discovered those naughty little boys had put stones in the line!

Danny also got ringworm on his head and told anyone that would listen he had "Animal-type Ring Worm." His father Foster (president of the local bank) was not thrilled at this announcement. When the neighbor died, Danny and Dennis ran chasing around outside loudly chanting, "Old Man Moore is Dead, Old Man Moore is Dead," much to their mother's chagrin. They were rather incorrigible and full of mischief.

Before the Daugherty family got television the twins came over to our house every Saturday to watch "The Big Top." We didn't have television until we moved to Constantine because my father's office machines had interfered with reception in the early days of TV. Once Danny was thought to be missing for hours! After much frantic searching in the neighborhood he was found so quietly sitting in front of our TV.

We had back alley neighbors that were very strict fundamental Christians. Their kids were not allowed to watch TV or go to movies. One of their daughters (Lois) was in my class at school. My father gave her free adjustments for her ailing back so she arranged to have them on Monday nights so she could sit with me and watch "I Love Lucy."

During 7th grade some of us girls formed a club called DYBA (Do Your Best Always) Other than having meetings and writing up our "minutes" I can't recall we did anything.

My best friend in class from seventh grade through high school was Barbara Baechler. We often even "double dated." At the beginning of our senior year we decided to try out together for the cheerleading team. Our routine even featured a cartwheel. We didn't make the squad (boo...hiss!). Barb later married Roger Daugherty. I was a bridesmaid at her wedding and she was a bridesmaid at my wedding. We were both married in the Methodist church in Constantine. Sadly, Roger died in November 2001. My husband and I were with Barb and Roger in Seattle, Washington on 9/11. Joy, Barb and I have remained friends and have gotten together several times since Roger died

Barb and Rog... January, 1955

After Dad gave me Laddie I had another really good buddy in high school. She lived in the country and also had a horse. Her name was Jonie Copenhaver. My dad once bought us dog collars to wear on our ankles....it was the latest rage! (As well as white buck shoes) Sometimes I rode horses with another friend who lived closer, Pat Rifenburg.

Also, before she moved from Constantine a gal named Mary Ellen McCuen rode her horse with me a lot. However she went to high school in the nearby town of White Pigeon and rivalry between our sports teams was fierce! Happily she and I both went to Albion College later where we became the best of friends again as well as sorority sisters.

Because I was an only child my parents were very indulgent about me having pets. I think my parents liked having them too. At one point I had Laddie, Sammy, a canary and a hamster all at once. One time the hamster (Hammy) was on my grandpa's shoulder when Grandpa Sid was half asleep. Hammy got brushed hard to the floor and ended up with a big swollen jaw. One time he went missing for days. We decided he had probably gone down the duct work and into the furnace. But one day my dad heard a child in his office waiting room saying, "Mother, there is a little rabbit in here." The mother replied "Don't be silly." My father dashed into the room and grabbed Hammy who had come out of one of the ducts! (My Dad's office was part of our house.) After the canary died we got a parakeet. Parakeets can repeat the letter "r" quite well. While I was in high school I had 3 boyfriends. The sequence was Richard, George, and Harry. Unfortunately the parakeet would learn one fellow's name and repeat it continuously after I had moved on to the next fellow. Fortunately none of them spoke bird talk. Pete the parakeet was still around when I went off to college.

I was now 14 and we went on a driving vacation out West to California. Vaughnie went with us. This time we didn't take Grandma and Grandpa as we had done on two previous vacations (One to Florida, one to Canada) One day we stopped for lunch and I discovered later I had left my prom photos at the restaurant 50 miles back...of course my Dad was furious and who could blame him, but Mother made him go back and get them! I am afraid I haven't changed much on leaving things!

We stopped on the way back in East Troy to see friends. My parent's friends Gib and Lila Tess had a basset hound. She had an "affair" with a beagle. You would think we would give up on having dogs, but no, we brought back a puppy. So now we had Gilbert, named after Gib. Gilbert lived to be about 15 years old (Yea!) and was well known around Birch Lake where my parents eventually bought a cottage when I was a junior in high school. He visited the girl scout camp often, begging treats, and was even known to grab a steak from a neighbor's grill. (The neighbor just brushed it off and served it up)

In addition to seeing Niagra Falls, two things stand out to me about the trip to Canada in 1950. One, my grandpa woke us at 2 AM announcing it was 7 AM and time to leave. When we were packed and Vaughnie and I were still laying in our clothes on the bed, Grandpa sat down on the rocking chair in the motel room and said, "Well you can all go back to sleep now, it is only 2AM." Everyone was really mad at him. The other thing is that when we were coming back across the border and they were checking us through, I said "They said be sure to tell the customs you belong to us," The custom officer got very suspicious and we had to open our suitcases and they went through everything. My Dad just glared at me.....well Dad told me to say that!!! It also rained the entire trip and we had many suitcases stacked on a carrier on top of the car. My Dad had to juggle the suitcases off and on every day.

An earlier trip to Florida (before we moved from East Troy) was memorable for visiting Cypress Gardens where we saw the beautiful gardens and wonderful water ski show (I love to water ski. That was an inspiration, for sure) and riding on the glass bottom boat at Silver Springs. As the tourists were looking down to see the fish under the boat a half dollar clanked on the glass. The "skipper" called out, "Hold your tips folks, hold your tips." My Dad, who had been watching him, whispered to Mom, "He tossed that coin himself to try to get everyone to tip him at the end of the ride." (Rather clever.)

Also particularly memorable was the day in New Orleans my Dad went the wrong way on a one way street. He couldn't turn around and every single driver that passed him on the narrow street yelled at him that he was going the wrong way (as though he wouldn't know it!!) Another thing I remember was that on that trip somewhere in the South my Dad left a pretty good tip for a "colored" waitress. My parents saw the proprietor go back and pick it up from the table so she couldn't have it. That was bad but Mom and Dad didn't know what to do about it.

I am not including much about my high school years in this particular memoir because it is long enough already!!

Chubby Stage
About 1950

Daugherty twins Danny and Dennis 1950

Christmas in Chicago 1951
Sandi, Mom, Vaughn, Grandma
Dwayne, Dwight, Butch, Aunt Helen and Uncle Merle

Grandpa. Mom and Dad Out on the Town
Chicago 1951 0r 1952

Laddie and Me
Summer 1951

Sammy and Me astride Laddie
This was my 1952
Christmas card photo

Our home in Constantine

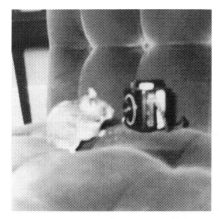 

Little Hammy isn't
camera shy

Sammy stares at Hammy
A standoff

Mom and Dad in the 50's

Freshman in High school
Before my pony tale
I loved that pearl collar
Teenage years; changes and challenges

Out West at Mom's Aunt Adella's
Me, Mom, Vaughn and Dad 1953

A favorite photo
Gilbert and me at our cottage at Birch Lake
1954? 1955?

Portraits when Mother was "Worthy Matron"
For Eastern Star. Around 1960

And her escort

This is a little sketch I did of Dad around 1984

Here is a poem I wrote about my Dad in about 1985

Reminiscing of days gone by
And thinking of my Dad
Reminds me of my childhood
And good times that we had

Squirming past Dad in our breakfast booth
During lunch I sat inside
Under the table and past his legs
Running back to play outside

Once when I ran in front of a truck
He spanked me very hard
And another time I disappeared with older kids
Off to the railroad yard

But Dad was always very kind
And thoughtfulness was his way
He got Mom a corsage and me one too
On Easter and Mother's Day

However, when I was very pokey
He'd say "Hustle Bustle Suds"
Or "Were you looking on the ceiling?"
When he'd find what I couldn't "Cause!"

Sunday fishing trips were lots of fun
Dad would bait the hook
Then sneak a bluegill on my line
While I read a comic book

Busy times at Christmas
With all his family
A quiet morning in a National park
A chipmunk at his knee

Wonderful trips as a child
Particularly out West!
The advantages he never had...
For me, he wanted the best

Leaving my prom pictures on a restaurant counter
(In Iowa)
Did cause him some chagrin
A hundred mile trip back and forth
I never did that again!

However I lost a sweater on a shopping trip
Dad didn't even complain
Just bought me one nicer (a Jansen, I think)
I hadn't even to explain

High school days in Constantine
(You came to my band concerts of course)
Remember the sock dog collars for Jonie and me?
You even bought me a horse

When Mom got very upset with me
Because on a report card I got a D
Dad said it really was OK
(It was the only time, you see)

Remember when the hamster got loose
And your patients thought it a mouse?
Hammy knew every bit of the ductwork
Back and forth in the house

During college days we almost missed
Theta's Father's Day BIG BOOM
Because his darling daughter
Got smoking in her room

Friends were always welcome
And CERTAINLY well fed
Kay and Johnnie came to welcome arms
(And even dear old Ted)

Golf tournament wins, Big Real Estate Sales
Wouldn't be the same
If I couldn't call my Dad to brag
To tell him of my "fame"

Doctor, Mayor, District Governor
Your accomplishments are great
But the really most important...
As a PERSON you really rate

You taught me pride
But not to be proud where others were concerned
Many, many subtle things
From my father I have learned

So many lovely memories
More than I can recall today
Stored up in the tapes inside my head
Will never fade away

My love that I have for you, Dear Dad
Is solid in my heart
You're a great source of strength to the whole family
That thought I must impart!

March 2, 2017...My mother would be 100 today!

Cecil John Dixon
October 18, 1912 –May 6, 1990

Mildred Edith Ellen Motley Dixon
March 2, 1917-February 14, 2008

Ogema
July 2008

Here I am with Rosie wearing Mom's old baggy clothes.
The house is sold and the auction is over.